Clyde's Leopard

Helen Dunmore

Illustrated by Gerry Ball

CAMBRIDGE
UNIVERSITY PRESS

Cambridge Reading

General Editors
Richard Brown and Kate Ruttle

Consultant Editor
Jean Glasberg

PUBLISHED BY THE PRESS SYNDICATE OF THE UNIVERSITY OF CAMBRIDGE
The Pitt Building, Trumpington Street, Cambridge CB2 1RP, United Kingdom

CAMBRIDGE UNIVERSITY PRESS
The Edinburgh Building, Cambridge CB2 2RU, United Kingdom
40 West 20th Street, New York, NY 10011-4211, USA
10 Stamford Road, Oakleigh, Melbourne 3166, Australia

First published 1998
Reprinted 1998

Printed in the United Kingdom at the University Press, Cambridge

Typeset in Concorde

A catalogue record for this book is available from the British Library

ISBN 0 521 63743 0 paperback

Other Cambridge Reading books you may enjoy

Tower Block Blowdown
J. Burchett and S. Vogler

Captain Cool and the Robogang
Gerald Rose

Don't Do That!
Helen Cook and Morag Styles

Leopard on the Mountain
Ruskin Bond

Other books by Helen Dunmore you may enjoy

Great-grandma's Dancing Dress

Amina's Blanket

Allie's Apples

Go Fox

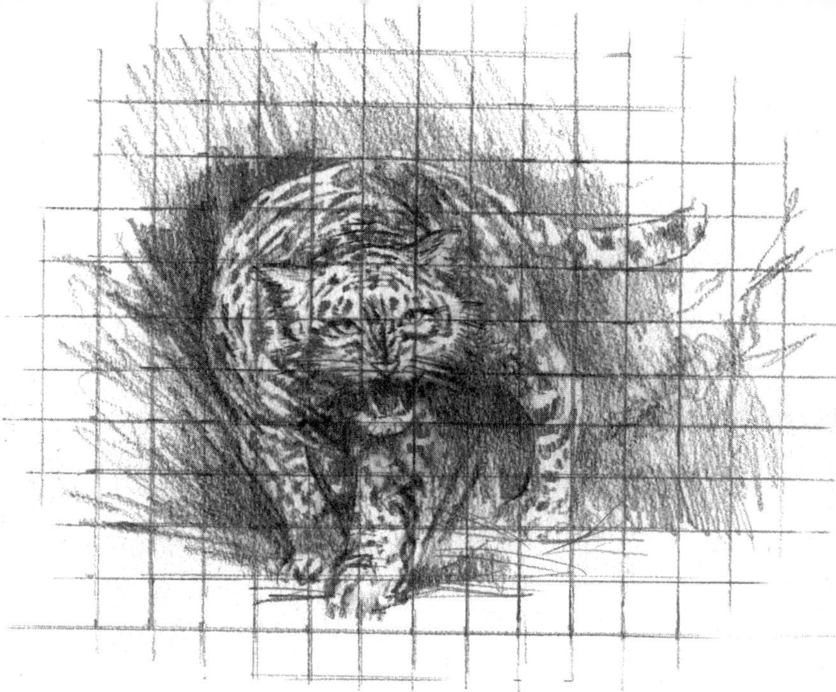

I was with Dad when I first saw the leopard.

"There's something wrong with that creature," Dad said. We stood in the rain and watched the leopard pacing up and down its cage, its tail twitching. Its head was down and it wasn't looking at anything. Suddenly, it banged against the wall as if it didn't know how big the cage was. The rain fell and it was getting dark, but I couldn't leave the leopard. It thudded into the side of the cage again, harder.

"Come on, Clyde. I don't know what you want to watch this for. Poor devil," said Dad.

I didn't want to watch. I had to. All that power in its muscles. Its sleek skin tight over its shoulders. I heard the leopard's claws scrape on the concrete floor of the cage as it turned, and then its tail was lashing from side to side.

"I'm going to get one of the keepers. There's something not right," Dad said. "You wait here a minute, Clyde." He went off. I didn't move. All I wanted was for the leopard not to be here, for this not to be happening. The cage clanged as the leopard jarred against it again. It was going to start throwing itself against the walls. It was going to beat itself against those walls until it died.

But it didn't, of course. The keeper came running with Dad, and Dad made me go away. When we were in the car, I said, "What'll they do to it, Dad? They won't kill it, will they?"

"No," Dad said, but he didn't sound too happy. "They'll dope it. Give it a tranquilliser. Leopards are valuable animals."

When I got home, I went to my room and lay on the bed. I felt like the leopard, full of anger, wanting to hit against something. But there was nothing to hit against. I reached down and picked my sketchbook up off the floor. I found a clean page and got my pack of drawing pencils.

I started to draw the cage. Thick black lines going down, one after another. And bushes all round that were meant to make the cage look less like a prison. Inside, I drew the leopard, cut into stripes by the bars of the cage. I drew its head hanging down, and its shoulder muscles bunched with tension. Then I pushed the drawing away and looked at it. It wasn't that good. It looked like any leopard in any cage. You couldn't see the anger. I flipped over to a clean page and began to draw again.

This time, the pencil knew what to do. I drew a tree, with thick twisted branches and a canopy of leaves. And on one of the thickest, strongest branches, I drew the leopard. It lay along the branch, its body melting into the pattern of the tree. You'd have to look twice to see it. If you were down on the ground, you'd never see it at all. The leopard lay as if it was part of the branch. Completely relaxed. But its head was up, watching, waiting. Any minute, that long, spotted body would pour off the branch and spring onto its prey. All around it, for miles and miles, there were trees and long, dry, golden grass. But I didn't draw all that, though I knew it was there. I just drew the leopard on its branch, waiting, watching. Ready to spring and run for miles if it wanted.

"Clyde!" shouted Mum from downstairs. "CLYDE!" Her voice sounded as though she'd been calling me for a long time.

I pushed the sketchbook under the bed and went down.

They'd been arguing again. The air was stiff with it. That was why Dad and I had gone to the zoo, because it was Sunday and if Mum and Dad did things together they always ended up arguing. I ate my pizza and I looked down at the table and thought of the leopard, bounding over the long, golden grass. I didn't hear anything they said.

That was last year, when I was still in Mr Davison's class. Things are different now. I don't do drawings any more.

I've been late a lot this term, but this morning I was really late. Registration was over, half the class was doing maths and the others were finishing their history reports. By the time Mrs Treece had stopped going on at me and I could slide into my chair, it was quarter to ten.

Matt looked up and said, "Did you hear about the wall?"

"No, what wall?"

"The playground wall's going to be painted. There's an artist coming to do a mural."

"Clyde! Please get your maths out and don't stop Matt working," said Mrs Treece. She was in a really bad mood. She'd already said she was going to get Mum to come in and talk to her about my being late, so I stopped talking and scrabbled round for my books.

But I couldn't think about maths. The ugly grey breeze-block playground wall lay across my mind. I couldn't imagine that wall with a painting on it.

"He's coming this afternoon," Matt whispered, without looking at me.

"The artist?"

"Yeah."

He came in an old white van with 'WASH ME' written in the dirt on the back. He was the tallest man I'd ever seen. When Mrs Treece stood next to him, her head only came up to his elbow. His eyes were very dark and shiny, looking down at us from high up.

"I'm Sam Florio," he said. "You can call me Sam." He wore a black leather jacket without a speck of paint on it. He looked more like a biker than an artist. We were out in the playground, by the wall.

"OK," he said, looking at us, then at the wall. "This is your wall, so I want your ideas." It was a sharp, sunny day and the wall looked uglier than ever. Kids like Ellie Jones and Jonathan Gore jumped about with their hands waving wildly and ideas bursting out of their mouths.

"We could have a rainforest background."

"We could have all the animals that people are killing off."

"Endangered species!" shouted Ellie Jones.

I looked away, over the top of the wall. The mural wasn't going to be anything to do with me.

Sam Florio took off his leather jacket and laid it on the ground at the foot of the wall.

"But what do *you* want?" he asked. "What do *you* like? Think about it." Slowly, slowly, his eyes moved from face to face until he was looking straight at me. What did I want? I didn't want to think about it. Dad once told me: never let anyone know what you really want, or they'll make sure you don't get it. Other kids' ideas went bouncing round the playground. Colours. Background. Big trees and birds like toucans and parrots. Colours flashing out against the green. There were too many ideas and I couldn't see how any of them could become real.

"But first of all," said Sam Florio, "we have to do the preparation. The boring bit, some people call it. I don't. This wall has to be scrubbed and primed or the paint won't last more than six months. It'll crack and come off the wall. Anyone who wants to help, I'd appreciate it."

I knew all about preparation. I used to help Dad in the holidays. Dad used the steam stripper to take off old wallpaper. I sanded and filled in holes. Sometimes, the person whose house we were working in brought tea for Dad and juice for me. That was before Mum told Dad to go.

Not many kids wanted to help with the preparation. They moaned that they wanted to do painting, not clean up a dirty old wall, so Mrs Treece said I could work on the wall all afternoon if I wanted. I could see her thinking it'd be less trouble if I was out there. Matt and Martina Foster wanted to help as well.

"Four of us is plenty," said Sam Florio. "I'd rather have the ones who really want to do it than the whole class out here mucking about. They'll all get a turn with the painting later on."

The wind was cold but the sun was bright and we soon got hot with working. I'd never seen anyone work faster than Sam Florio, not even Dad. Maybe it was being so tall. His hands were long and strong and sure. They scraped and scrubbed and primed like the hands of five men. The closer I got to the ugly old breeze-block wall, the more I got to like it. I was beginning to see just how good it would look once it was painted. I liked the steady way we worked, with the sound of scrapers and the smell of priming paint all round us. If I shut my eyes I could almost believe that Dad was working beside me.

"Take a break," said Sam Florio, as one of the kids from Class 4 came slowly across the playground, carrying a wobbly tray with mugs of tea.

"Is that tea for us as well?" asked Matt.

"Sure. You've been working, the same as me."

I spooned sugar into my mug of tea, the way Dad always did. You need sugar for energy when you're working. There was a packet of ginger biscuits too. Sam Florio looked along the wall, inspecting the work, while we ate biscuits and drank tea.

"Soon have this finished," he said. "I'll work on it till it gets dark, after you lot go home. Tomorrow it'll be dry."

And then Ellie Jones and Jonathan Gore and the rest of them will be out here painting their ideas onto it, I thought. It won't be our wall any more.

"That question I asked you," said Sam Florio. "Have you got an answer yet?"

"What question?" asked Martina.

"What do you want on this wall?"

"An anaconda," said Matt. It was true, I knew it. Matt loved snakes. He was saving up for a snake of his own, to keep in a glass box in his bedroom.

"So, you'd like an anaconda on the wall?" asked Sam Florio. "Sounds OK to me. It's a long time since I had the chance to draw an anaconda."

Matt looked at me. It was a 'Go on, you say something now' look.

"Not a snake for you," said Sam Florio, looking at me.

"No," I said.

"Clyde can draw," said Martina suddenly. "He used to do brilliant drawings when we were in Mr Davison's class.

I felt Sam Florio looking at me, but I wasn't going to look back. Brilliant drawings. I thought of the big green sketchbook Dad had bought me. "Maybe you'll be an architect one day," Dad had said. "They have to be good at drawing." But I hadn't touched the book since last year.

Brilliant drawings. It felt as though someone else had done them. When Mrs Treece gave out paints and paper, or drawing pencils, my hands just wouldn't work any more. But out here, in the sun, in front of the playground wall that was just waiting for paint, maybe, maybe . . .

"Tomorrow I'll start to draw the design onto the wall," said Sam Florio. "I'll be working on the design tonight, after I've finished here. See this notebook?" He tapped it. "All your ideas are in here." He snapped open the notebook and wrote down 'Anaconda'. Then he put the notebook back down on the ground, in the pocket of his leather jacket.

"I'm going in for five minutes," he said.

"Can we go to the toilet now?" asked Matt.

"Go ahead."

Matt and Martina followed Sam Florio across the playground, but I stayed where I was. The door into school swung shut behind them. I was alone, with the high grey wall in front of me. Cleaning it and priming it had changed things. It wasn't just part of the school now. It belonged to me as well.

I looked all around, then I bent down quickly and felt inside Sam Florio's leather jacket. There was the notebook. I flipped open the pages. They were covered in words and tiny drawings: a football boot kicking a ball, a girl running, the long branches of a tree brushing the ground. They must be drawings from other murals he'd done. They were good. I turned the pages until I found a clean one. There was a little pencil in the spine of the notebook. I took it out and looked round again. Then I crouched down with the book on my knee, took a deep breath, and drew.

It only took a few minutes. By the time Matt and Martina came out, the notebook was back in Sam Florio's jacket pocket.

The next morning, I got in early and went straight to the wall. Sam was there, drawing squares all over it.

"This is how I transfer the design," he said. "Each square on the wall matches a square on my design. It's all measured out. This way all the trees and animals should come out in the right places on the wall."

"Can we see your design?" asked Ellie Jones, looking at the roll of paper that lay on the ground.

"Not yet," said Sam. "You'd better go on in now."

It was time for registration, but I stayed there, watching. Sam was numbering the squares. Then he stepped back to look at the wall, and saw that I was still there.

"Want to see the design?"

"I don't mind."

He bent down and unrolled the paper. "I've done a colour sketch too. This is the black and white one that we use to help us get the drawing onto the wall." The wind snatched at the paper as Sam smoothed it and spread it out. "There."

There was a background of thick trees, with twisted, muscly trunks and branches. There were toucans and parrots and an anaconda coiled up like a heap of rope. There were wild tangles of creeper and sploshes of flowers. It was good. Really good. The drawing was divided into tiny numbered squares, to match those on the wall.

The left-hand part of the roll of paper had curled up again. Sam spread it out and held it down.

“Look,” he said. I looked, then looked again. On the thickest, most twisted branch, there was a shape I knew. It lay there as if it had been poured onto the branch. Relaxed, as if it was sleeping. But it wasn’t sleeping. The tip of its tail seemed to quiver with life. I could almost see it switch from side to side as it waited, waited . . .

My leopard.

"Nice piece of drawing," said Sam.

"Yeah, it's good," I said.

He turned and looked straight at me. "I meant yours," he said. "The leopard. All I've done is copy the drawing you did in my notebook, and scale it up. See those squares on the wall? 23, 24 and 25, and 39, 40 and 41. That's where your leopard's going to go."

I looked at the drawing, then at the wall. I could see just where the leopard would be, lying along the thick branch that twisted out of the canopy of trees. Hidden, until you looked twice.

"Here," said Sam. He had a lump of chalk in his hand. "Have a go. This wipes straight off if you don't like what you've done. See if you can scale up the drawing so it goes in the right place."

He made it sound as though it was the easiest thing in the world. But my hand was clumsy as I took the chalk. Maybe I couldn't do it any more, not with him watching.

"It's your leopard," said Sam. "You know him better than anyone else."

And suddenly I knew I could do it. He was my leopard. He was waiting, and the wall was waiting. I touched the chalk to the surface of the wall. It made a sudden mark, like a shout in silence.

"Go on. Look at the drawing, then go for it."

And the chalk started to move. Once I began, it was like swimming. Once you've learnt to swim, you can't forget.

The leopard grew under my hand. His long, rippling back, his huge cat head. He lay along the branch as if he'd been born there. Any moment now he would spring off the branch. I stood back. He was there. The drawing had worked.

"That's fine," said Sam.

All the breath I'd been holding went out in a sigh. It felt as though something was finished, even though I knew the real work had only just begun. The whole design had to be transferred onto the wall, and outlined in something that would last better than chalk if it rained. And then there'd be all the painting, with some kids being stupid and slopping paint around, and others only caring about their own bit, not about anyone else's. But I knew Sam wouldn't let them muck about with my leopard.

"It's a big job," said Sam, "but we've made a start."

I was going to be late, really late. "I've got to go in," I said, and picked up my bag.

"See you later," said Sam. I ran across the

playground and pulled open the door. Then I looked back. Sam had started work again. Most of the wall was dull grey, ugly if you didn't know it close up. But I knew that wall now, every inch of it. And even from right across the playground I could see my leopard lying across its branch, ready to spring.